101 Coolest Things to Do in Poland

Introduction

So you're going to Poland, huh? You lucky lucky thing! You are sure in for a treat because Poland is, without a doubt, one of the most special travel destinations in Europe – the world even! It offers something for every visitor, so whether you are into exploring the local gastronomic scene, ogling at ancient fortresses and palaces, or meeting locals on the party scene, this country has something that you'll treasure.

This guide will take you on a journey to all the hotspots of Poland like Krakow, Warsaw, Wroclaw, Poznan, Gdansk, Zakopane, and many other places besides.

In this guide, we'll be giving you the low down on:
- the very best things to shove in your pie hole, whether you want to chow down on traditional pierogis or you want to indulge at an authentic vodka bar
- incredible festivals, from electronic festivals with world famous headliners through to a vodka festival where you can really let loose

- the coolest historical and cultural sights that you simply cannot afford to miss like the largest castle in the whole world, and world class galleries
- the most incredible outdoor adventures, whether you want to raft through a gorgeous river gorge or you fancy a snowboarding adventure in Zakopane
- where to shop for authentic souvenirs so that you can remember your trip to Poland forever
- the places where you can party like a local and make new friends
- and tonnes more coolness besides!

Let's not waste any more time – here are the 101 coolest things not to miss in Poland!

1. Stroll the Pines of the Crooked Forest

Poland is a country that is full of fairy tale landscapes, but the Crooked Forest is more like Alice in Wonderland meets the Twilight Zone. This forest is located in a tiny corner of west Poland, and what makes it special are the 400 pine trees that have a remarkable 90 degree bend right at the bases of their trunks. It is thought the that weird curved trunks were caused by human intervention, but nobody is quite sure how it was done, or what the reasoning behind it was. *(74-100 Nowe Czarnowo)*

2. Go Underground at the Wieliczka Salt Mine

One of the most popular day trips from Krakow is a visit to the Wieliczka Salt Mine, and it's with good reason. Head underground and you'll be immersed in a world of pits and chambers that have all been carved out of salt. As well as a wonder for the eyes, the salt mine is visited for its microclimate and its health giving properties as it's been known to rid people of very serious allergies. There's even an ornamented church down there!

(Daniłowicza 10, 32-020 Wieliczka; ww.kopalnia.pl)

3. Visit Poland's Most Important Church, Wawel Cathedral

Poland is a country that has no shortage of stunning church architecture, but there is one church that stands head and shoulders above the rest in terms of its importance and beauty: the Wawel Cathedral in Krakow. Why so important? This church is over 900 years old and it's the place where most of the former Polish Royal monarchs had their coronation. Head into the Royal Crypts to see the grandeur of the former monarch's tombs and gilded coffins.

(Wawel 3, 31-001 Kraków; www.katedra-wawelska.pl)

4. Discover 1000 Years of Jewish History in Warsaw

When many people think of the lives of Jewish people in Poland, they would think of the atrocities that happened during the Second World War. But before that, there were Jews living in Warsaw for 1000 years, and you can get an insight into that history at the Museum of Polish Jews in the city. The impressive exhibition consists of a multimedia narrative with paintings, oral guides, and interactive installations that tell the history of ordinary lives within the city of Warsaw.

(Anielewicza 6, 00-157 Warszawa; www.polin.pl)

5. Feel the Charm of a Painted Village Called Zalipie

If you really want to get off the beaten track while you're in Poland, be sure to make the time to visit lesser known towns and villages. The village of Zalipie is a perfect example of Polish charm that many tourists don't get to see. It's often described as the most beautiful village in Poland, and this is because of its delightful wooden cottages, each of which is hand painted with colourful floral motifs that can make it seem as though you are inside the pages of a fairy tale.

6. Say Hi to the Animals at Wroclaw Zoo

One of the most delightful things that you can do with a free day is visit a local zoo, and say hi to all kinds of animals. When in Poland, the best zoo to visit is Wroclaw Zoo, and this also happens to be the oldest zoo in the country. In fact, it dates all the way back to 1865 when Wroclaw was a part of Prussia. Over 1,100 different species are represented, and you'll have the chance to get close to animals like manatees, crocodiles, penguins, and much more.

(Wróblewskiego 1-5, 51-618 Wrocław; www.zoo.wroclaw.pl)

7. Have a Retro Milk Bar Experience in Warsaw

Want to have an authentic dining experience while you're in Poland? Have a limited budget but still want to eat out? Then you absolutely need to know about and frequent a few Milk Bars. These Milk Bars date back to Communist era Poland when the government opened these eateries to serve hordes of mass workers. These days, they are still a place to get a humble, normally dairy based meal, at a cheap price. There are so many cheap, good quality Milk Bars in Warsaw that it's worth walking around and eating in every one that you can find.

8. Feel the Grandeur of Wawel Royal Castle

If you want to get an idea of the political and cultural history and influence of the monarchs in Poland, it's essential that you visit the Wawel Royal Castle in Krakow. The palace that you see today dates back to the 16th century, and is split into five different museums. If you only have time for one, make sure that you check out the State Rooms and Royal Private Apartments, which have their original larch wood ceilings, pained wall friezes, stunning Renaissance furniture and artworks.

(Wawel 5, 31-001 Kraków; www.wawel.krakow.pl/en)

9. Warm Yourself With Polish Plum Brandy, Sliwowica

One of the most pleasing things to do in a new country is try their tipple of choice. We're pretty sure that Polish vodka is already on your radar, but something that you might not know is that Poland also creates its own plum brandy, and it's totally delicious. This is strong stuff, but is very drinkable because of its fruitiness. And without a doubt, it's the best way to warm yourself through if you visit Poland during its colder months.

10. Geek Out in Krakow's Pharmacy Museum

The idea of a pharmacy museum might not sound all that exciting, but this is one of the largest museums of its type anywhere in the world, and is totally fascinating whether you're an A-Grade Science Geek or not. There's a staggering 22,000 items in their collection, and you'll be able to explore old lab equipment, rare pharmaceutical instruments, stoneware, glassware, medical documents, and loads more besides.

(Floriańska 25, 31-019 Kraków; http://muzeumfarmacji.pl)

11. Pay Your Respects at Auschwitz Concentration Camp

One of the Polish places of interest that everybody seems to know about, and for the saddest and most tragic reasons, is Auschwitz Concentration Camp. During the Second World War, around 11 million people died at this Nazi camp. Today the grounds are a memorial to those who suffered and were killed at the hands of Nazis in Auschwitz and other concentration camps around Poland. It's a sombre place, but sometimes travel can do the really important task of highlighting what we value and want from the world we live in, and what we cannot tolerate.

(http://auschwitz.org/en/visiting)

12. Take in the Fairytale Gothic Architecture of Ksiaz Castle

Make your way to the small city of Walbrzych in southern Poland, look across the hills, and your heart will suddenly start to fill at the gorgeous sight of the unbelievably beautiful Ksiaz Castle. This castle dates all the way back to the late 13th century, and has been modified through the centuries so that it has features of Gothic, Baroque, and Rococo design. The somewhat sinister side to the castle is that it was being eyed up by Adolf Hitler as his future residence.

(Piastów Śląskich 1, 58-306 Wałbrzych; www.ksiaz.walbrzych.pl)

13. Dance to World Class Bands at Orange Warsaw Festival

Polish people definitely know how to party, and we think that can be huge amounts of fun to try and keep up with their pace at one of Poland's epic summer festivals. The Orange Warsaw Festival is hosted each year in early June, and it's a huge crowd pleaser with popular music names that attracts around 50000 guests each year. Some of the artists that have performed in previous years include Kings of Leon, Kasabian, and David Guetta.

(https://orangewarsawfestival.pl)

14. Enter an Upside Down House in Szymbark

Part tourist attraction and part political symbol, the upside down house in Szymbark is one of the more unusual things that you are likely to set your eyes on while you travel around Poland. The house was constructed in 2007 and is purposely upside down in order the represent the inversions and back to front logic of communist rule. You will have to climb through the attic windows, walk on the ceiling, and check out the Soviet furnishings.

15. Treat Yourself to Plenty of Babka

If you have something of a sweet tooth, fear not because there is plenty that you can get indulgent with in Poland. One of our favourite Polish sweet treats is traditionally served on Easter Sunday, but realistically it can be found at any time of the year – and that is babka. Babka is a spongey, yeast enriched cake that has a tall cylindrical form and is often served with a chocolate sauce.

16. Get Colourful at Warsaw's Neon Museum

In the first half of the twentieth century, Poland was a particularly grey looking place. But following the death of Stalin in the 1950s, there was an active program of "neonisation" that was tasked with brightening up the country. In Warsaw's Neon Museum, you can check out hundreds of neon signs that were put up across Poland from the 1950s to the 1970s. It's a fascinating insight into the cultural and design history of a nation.

(Mińska 25, Soho Factory, 03-804 Warszawa; www.neonmuzeum.org)

17. Discover Historic Scientific Instruments at Collegium Maius

Krakow is a city that is absolutely bursting full with historic attractions, and history buffs should be sure to visit Collegium Maius, the oldest building of the Jagiellonian University, dating back to the 14th century. Wander around and you will find lecture rooms, university halls, a library, and a treasury. It's also home to a remarkable number of historic scientific instruments, as well as globes, furniture, coins, and many other exciting objects.

(Jagiellońska 15, 31-010 Kraków; www.maius.uj.edu.pl)

18. Take a Pilgrimage to the Holy Mountain of Grabarka

Although only 1% of Polish people belong to the Orthodox faith, Orthodox Christianity has had a significant effect on the country. Look to the Holy Mountain of Grabarka, which is completely covered in crosses of all shapes and sizes, and this will start to register as reality. Each year on August 18th and 19th, 10,000 believers take a pilgrimage to the mountain to pray and have an all night vigil of healing.

19. Spot the Wroclaw Dwarves Around the City

Wroclaw, for us, is one of the most picturesque and charming cities in the whole country - but it's also just a little bit strange. When you find your way to Wroclaw, look out for the little dwarf figurines that appear all over the streets. In 2001, a monument of a small dwarf was unveiled, and it represented an Anti-Communist group, but since then unofficial hordes of dwarves have virtually taken over the city. There are now 350 of them – can you spot them all?

20. Chow Down at the Good Taste Festival in Poznan

Ask us what our favourite thing to do when visiting a new country is, and we'll tell you that stuffing our face with food is normally the way to go. We love to go to cafes and restaurants, but we get specially excited at food festivals, where you can try loads of different foods you've never tried before, and all in one place. This international food show has culinary workshops, competitions, lots to buy and try, and even concerts. It takes place in August each year.

21. Discover Communist-era Posters at the Warsaw Poster Museum

Located inside the gorgeous Wilanow Palace complex in Warsaw, the Warsaw Poster Museum is the oldest poster museum in the whole world. When the museum opened back in the 1960s, it contained a collection of around 13,000 posters, but now it's home to more than 55,000, and there is a particular focus placed on

Communist era propaganda. It's also home to the biannual International Poster Biennale.

(Stanisława Kostki Potockiego 10/16, 02-958 Warszawa; www.postermuseum.pl)

22. Experience Total Relaxation at Uniejow Thermal Park

Poland is a country with so many things to see and so much to do, but sometimes you just need to relax, take it easy, and treat yourself, right? Well, where better to do so than in the country's oldest thermal spa, Uniejow? The whole complex is pumped full of geo-thermal water that's the perfect temperature for relaxation or a warm swim. There's even a beach, pier, and swim-up bar if you are there in the summer months.

(Zamkowa 3/5, 99-210 Uniejów; www.termyuniejow.pl)

23. Explore the Mysterious Odry Stone Circles

For history buffs, there is plenty to explore all over Poland. But look beyond the churches and castles, and you can even get a glimpse into the country's prehistory. The Odry Stone Circles are a group of stone monuments set into a circle in the central town of Odry. They date to the time of the Goths, which would be the 1st or 2nd century, and are Europe's second largest collection of ancient circles left intact. Some visitors report a sense of flowing calm and positive energy when they are on this ancient site.

24. Eat Fresh Obwarzanek From the Streets of Krakow

Our favourite way to explore a new city is to simply eat our way through everything in sight, and when in Krakow, obwarzanek is the way to go. This is a braided ring shaped bread that is braided, boiled, baked, and covered in salt and poppy seeds. In other words, it's a bagel, but we promise you that they really are something special in Krakow, and you can find street vendors selling them all over the city. They have actually been a daily sight on the central market square for 600 years.

25. Try Your Hand at Windsurfing in Jurata

Poland has earned a reputation as a travel destination with gorgeous religious architecture, friendly locals, and great parties, but what if you're an adventurer who likes to get outside and enjoy the best that the natural world has to offer? Poland doesn't disappoint in that respect either. Find your way to Jurata, a very charming seaside resort, because this is the place to enjoy activities on the water, and the windsurfing is especially good there if you want something to really get your heart pumping.

26. Warm Yourself With a Hot Beer From Eszeweria

There are two things that you really need to know about Poland. First of all, that you'll need to pack your woollens if you travel in the winter, because this country really does get cold. Secondly, that Poles love to drink beer. Put the two together and what do you get? Warm beer! And we're not talking about beer that's been left out of the fridge, but is actually served hot on purpose. Eszeweria is a lovely little bar in

Krakow that serves up warm beer as a specialty. And if you're there in the summer, check out their lush garden space.

(Józefa 9, 31-056 Kraków)

27. Discover Folk Art at the Ethnographic Museum of Wroclaw

The Ethnographic Museum of Wroclaw is certainly not the best known attraction or museum in the city, but we still that that it's worth a couple of hours of your time. What we really love is that it lets its wonderful objects teach you about the history of the city rather than giving you a tiresome history lesson. Inside you'll find some wonderful folk art, vintage dolls, national costumes, carvings, handicrafts, and more treats besides.

(Romualda Traugutta 111/113, 50-001 Wrocław; www.muzeumetnograficzne.pl)

28. Start a Night of Partying With a Mad Dog Shot

If you really want to travel like a local, then you have to drink like a local, and in Poland this can be quite the challenge because the local population sure does like a drink (or five). On the student scene, there is only one way to start an epic night out, and that's with a Mad Dog shot. So what does it contain? Vodka, of course! But also raspberry syrup and some droplets of tobasco sauce. It's fiery, fruity, and strong.

29. Warm Yourself With a Big Bowl of Bigos

If you find yourself in Poland during the cold, winter months, you'll surely want to take every opportunity to eat lots of comfort food that will want warm you from the inside out. And one of the heartiest local dishes is called bigos. This is a stew of finely chopped meat (and the meats can be of all kinds: beef, pork, chicken and veal), that is mixed with sauerkraut and topped with fresh cabbage. Some other ingredients that add flavour to the dish include cloves, caraway, garlic, marjoram, mustard seeds, and juniper berries.

30. Get Beer Happy at the Wroclaw Good Beer Festival

As you might expect, the Wroclaw Good Beer Festival is somewhere that beer lovers will feel right at home. Of course, you'll have the opportunity to sip on lots of local beers, but the festival packs in way more fun than just that. You can expect live music that's typical of the Lower Silesian region, food stalls so that you can line your stomach before taking in all that beer, and even some brewing workshops. It's hosted at the beginning of June.

(www.festiwaldobregopiwa.pl)

31. Hike to the Gorgeous Morskie Oko Lake

Poland is not just a country with gorgeous churches and town squares, it's also somewhere where you can immerse yourself in greenery and get back to nature. For total peace and tranquillity in a glorious setting, we are completely enamoured with Morskie Oko lake, which is located deep within Tatra National Park. It's a lovely hike from Zakopane to reach the lake, and it's different in every season. We particularly like the falling leaves of autumn.

32. Eat at Poland's First Restaurant With a Michelin Star

When you think of incredible world renowned restaurants that have earned Michelin stars, you'd probably first think of Paris or New York. But there is some great food to be had in Poland, and the Atelier Amaro restaurant is Warsaw is the very first eatery in the country to earn a Michelin star. Pay a visit, and you'll soon understand why. The food here is innovative and theatrical, and still delicious. Think snails served with asparagus in a smoke filled jar. *(Agrykola 1, 00-460 Warszawa; http://atelieramaro.pl)*

33. Go Gingerbread Crazy at the Torun Gingerbread Museum

Torun is a small city in northern Poland that is best known for its great love of gingerbread. Of course, we'd recommend that you put plenty of gingerbread in your mouth while you're in Torun, but also that you visit the Torun Gingerbread Museum, which is so much more than another stuffy museum. First of all, you'll actually be taught how to make gingerbread dough from the Middle Ages, and then you can cut out gingerbread shapes using traditional moulds.

(Rabiańska 9, 87-100 Toruń; https://muzeumpiernika.pl)

34. Traverse the World's Largest Ice Maze in Zakopane

The best place for winter activities and icy landscapes in Poland is most definitely Zakopane. It's well kitted out for activities like skiing and snowboarding, but for something a little different, be sure to check out the local ice maze, which is actually the largest ice maze in all of Poland. The maze takes up an astonishing 2500 square metres of space, and it's the perfect place to have some fun in the snow if you're travelling with kids.

35. Take in all the Grandeur of Wilanow Palace

Stand in front of the Wilanow Palace in Warsaw and you can't help but be blown away by all of its glistening majesty and grandeur. It dates all the way to 1677 when it was the residence of King Jan III Sobieski, but it has changed hand many times since then, and each of the owners has stamped their own Baroque features on to the place. We think you should carve out a whole day to stroll the grand halls and state rooms, with their lavishing furnishings and valuable paintings.

(Stanisława Kostki Potockiego 10/16, 02-958 Warszawa; www.wilanow-palac.pl)

36. Explore a Church Decorated With Thousands of Skulls

If you are a fan of church architecture and solemn spaces, Poland is brimming full with them, and one of the most unique of the bunch is Kaplica Czaszec, a church that is decorated with thousands upon thousands of skulls. During the Thirty Years War and the Seven Year War there were many mass graves. And a local grave digger took the remains of 3000 bodies from these graves in the 18th century, and decorated the walls and ceilings with them in a variety of patterns and cross formations. It's eerie but a must-see.

(Stanisława Moniuszki 8, 57-350 Kudowa-Zdró; www.czermna.pl)

37. Indulge a Music Fan at the Chopin Museum

If you are a person who loves classical music, you'll no doubt be familiar with the works of Frederic Chopin. Chopin was born and grew up in Warsaw, and this is a matter of intense pride for the local population. If you'd like to know more about the man and his life in Poland, be sure to visit the Chopin Museum, which has an incredible collection of manuscripts and documents written by the composer, photos and sculptures of him, and some of his letters. Check the museum's programme of events if you'd like to catch a live recital.

(Pałac Gnińskich, 00-368, Okólnik 1, 00-368 Warszawa; http://chopin.museum/en/information/visitors/id/222)

38. Learn Something New at the National Museum in Warsaw

For history buffs, a trip to the National Museum in Warsaw is most definitely in order. This wonderful place has been open since way back in 1862, and has grown in size and stature since then to become one of the most important museums in the whole country. There's a huge range of exhibits and objects, so there is bound to be something that gets you excited. From 15th century Dutch and Flemish paintings through to Medieval Nubian paintings, there is plenty to explore. *(Aleje Jerozolimskie 3, 00-495 Warszawa; www.mnw.art.pl)*

39. Take in a Show at the Gdansk Shakespeare Theatre

If you want to see a Shakespeare show, you so wouldn't think that Poland is the place to be, but Poland is a country with many cultural interests and you can even find a Shakespeare Theatre in Gdansk. There are performances in the original form of Shakespeare's English and also in Polish. And there is even a Shakespeare Festival in the summer that grips all the arts lovers of Gdansk.

(Wojciecha Bogusławskiego 1, 80-818 Gdańsk;
http://teatrszekspirowski.pl)

40. Discover Medieval Poland at Rynek Underground

Rynek Underground is a fairly recent addition to Krakow's museum scene, and it's well worth a visit to have an experience of Poland's Middle Ages meets the 21st century. The whole thing is underground and you'll be guided through a labyrinth of Medieval markets and chambers that are populated with holograms that bring the space to life in a very modern way. You'll also be transported to a different world via smoke machine, lasers, and 3 dimensional models of objects that can be manipulated via touchscreens.

(Rynek Główny 1, 33-332 Kraków;
http://podziemiarynku.com)

41. Get to Grips With the Polish Language

If you are planning an extended trip to Poland, it is well worth spending a bit of time at a Polish language school, particularly if you want to get off the beaten path and visit some places where English won't be widely spoken. There are some truly fantastic language schools right around the country but we are totally enamoured by the GLOSSA Polish Langauge School in Krakow thanks to its incredible teachers and intensive, immersive approach to language learning.

(Dietla 103, 31-031 Kraków; www.glossa.pl)

42. Party on the North Coast During Open'er Festival

Gdynia is a port city on the northern coast of Poland that rarely attracts tourists. That is, apart from when the annual Open'er Festival takes place there every July. What we really love about this festival is its inclusive spirit and how all kinds of different music are represented, so whether you are a rock, pop, or dance music fan, there will be something for you to get down to. Some artists that have taken to the stage of Open'er include Kasabian, Drake, and Radiohead.

(http://opener.pl/en)

43. Catch a Performance by the Polish Baltic Philharmonic

For fans of classical music, there is plenty to enjoy in Poland, and we would grab the opportunity to watch a performance by the Polish Baltic Philharmonic with both hands. This is the largest orchestra in northern Poland, and they even have their own concert venue, which is perched right on the edge of the Motlawa River in Gdansk.

(O łowianka 1, 80-001 Gdańsk; www.filharmonia.gda.pl)

44. Indulge a Sweet Tooth With Polish Paczki Doughnuts

It seems like no matter where you travel in the world, every country has its own version of the humble doughnut, and Poland is no exception. The Polish doughnut is called a Paczki, and anyone with a sweet tooth will fall in love with them. Unlike regular doughnuts, paczkis have alcohol in the dough to stop oil from seeping in so they stay fluffy. Sometimes they are yeasted, and they are filled with fruit jams, creams, and topped with powdered sugar and sometimes orange peel.

45. Go Kayaking on the Rospuda River

For nature lovers, one of the hidden treasures of Poland is the small Rospuda River, which is tucked away in the northeast country. This is a place mostly undiscovered by tourists, but it's perfect for scenic kayak trips that will have you completely stunned by Poland's beauty. You'll be completely surrounded by forest with clear waters beneath you so that you can experience the tranquillity of a different side of Poland.

46. Explore all the Beauty of Lodz's Botanical Garden

If you love nothing more than to surround yourself in natural beauty, be sure to make your way to the botanical gardens of Lodz, which are well regarded as the most impressive gardens in all of Poland. This 64 hectare site contains an array of different gardens in various styles such as a Japanese garden, a rock garden, and even a rural farmstead and cottage that you can visit. The botanists there are also happy to give gardening advice so don't be afraid to ask questions. *(Krzemieniecka 36/38, 94-303 Łódź; www.botaniczny.lodz.pl/en)*

47. Eat Pierogis Until You Burst

If there's one food that typifies the gastronomic culture of Poland it's the pierogi, and if you aren't familiar, this is the Polish take on a dumpling. They can be found all over Poland, and you'll find them sold pretty much everywhere – from street vendors, to casual cafes, to fine dining restaurants. The nice thing about pierogis is that they can be filled with all manner of things. Veggies will enjoy mashed potato and sauerkraut, while meat lovers can get into minced pork.

48. Listen to Baltic Music at the Sounds of the North Festival

When you think of summer festivals, you probably think of waving your hands in the air and dancing to electronic music, but if you'd like to experience something a little tamer, and that represents the culture of Poland better, you should know about the Sounds of the North Festival. This festival is hosted in Gdansk every two years, and it's the place to get to grips with the traditional folk music of the Baltic region.

49. Sample Some Great Vodka at Wodka Café Bar

A trip to Poland without visiting a vodka bar is not a trip to Poland at all in our opinion. Of course, you'll have no shortage of options to choose from when you want a stuff drink and some great company, but we are totally in love with the Wodka Café Bar, which is located in Krakow. This is a teeny tiny bar, but the selection is impressive, and the staff really know their stuff. We recommend ordering a flight so you can really get to grips with the local vodka culture.

(Mikołajska 5, 31-027 Kraków; http://wodkabar.pl)

50. Learn About the Nazi Occupation of Krakow at Schindler's Factory

If you have seen the movie, Schindler's List, you'll know that Schindler's Factory was a very important place. It was a site of resistance against the Nazis during their occupation of Krakow, when Oskar Schindler tried to protect the lives of his Jewish employees. Today, you can visit the administrative centre of the factory, where you can get to grips with what life was like for Krakow and its inhabitants during World War II.

(Lipowa 4F, 30-702 Kraków; www.mhk.pl/branches/oskar-schindlers-factory)

51. Head to Kasprowy Peak for an Adventure on the Ski Slopes

It's no secret that Poland can get more than a little bit chilly in the winter months, but the good news is that the chilly weather creates a veritable paradise for winter sports enthusiasts. Whether you are a newbie to skiing or an advanced skier, we'd definitely recommend Kasprowy peak in the famous resort town of Zakopane. No artificial snow is ever used here so you can guarantee you'll be getting the authentic winter adventure experience

52. Snuggle up to Kitties at Krakow Cat Café

When you think of Cat Cafes, you would probably think of Asian cities like Tokyo or Taipei, but believe it or not, there is now a Cat Café in Krakow as well. The idea is simple. While you sip on your latte or green tea, you'll be immersed in a world of kitties that will want to snuggle up against you, and what could be cuter than that?

(Krowoderska 48, 31-158 Kraków;
http://kociakawiarniakrakow.pl)

53. Watch the World Go By in Poznan's Old Town Square

Poland is a country that is full of all kinds of excitement, but it can be also nice to have some lazy afternoons that consist of nothing more than sipping on coffee in a beautiful location and watching the world go by. When we're in that kind of mood, it's always the small and overlooked city of Poznan that takes our fancy. The Old Market Square is simply stunning, with historic tenement houses, and many quaint restaurants and cafés lining the square.

54. Feel Festive at Wroclaw's Christmas Market

Okay, we know that visiting Poland in the winter is a bit of an ask because of the nail bitingly cold weather, but just think of how festive Poland's historic cities look in December! And Poland is also a fantastic destination for various Christmas markets, but the crowning glory has to be the annual Wroclaw Christmas market. The market square comes to life with festive decorations, and wooden stalls selling decorations, Christmas food, and more. Be sure to treat yourself to chocolate gingerbread cookies and mulled wine.

55. Stroll the Manicured Lawns of Lazienki Park

As the capital city of Poland, Warsaw is a place with many buildings and honking cars. This can be overwhelming if you are not used to city life, but fear not because Warsaw also happens to be a very green city. When you need an escape, just find your way to Lazienki Park, which is the largest green space in Warsaw. The gardens date all the way back to the 17th century. On top of lots of greenery, you'll find a palace, a classical amphitheatre, and an astronomical observatory.

(www.lazienki-krolewskie.pl)

56. Enjoy Some Smooth Sounds at Warsaw Summer Jazz Days

If you are a jazz lover through and through, Poland probably wouldn't be your first choice of destination for a holiday filled with the smooth sounds of Jazz, but actually, Warsaw plays host to one of the most popular summer jazz festivals in Europe: Warsaw Summer Jazz Days. The festival either takes place at the end of June or beginning of July, and culminates in a huge open-air jazz party in Zamkowy Square.

(http://warsawsummerjazzdays.pl)

57. Slurp on a Unique Soup Called Zurek

When you need to put something into your body that will warm you from the inside out, we recommend a hearty bowl of Zurek, which is otherwise known as sour rye soup. This soup is made of soured rye flour (in the same way that sourdough is soured), and meat, which would usually pieces of boiled pork sausage. The soup is often served in an edible bowl made of bread.

58. Indulge an Inner Child at Poland's Largest Toy Museum

There are times in life when you just have to forget about the stresses of daily life, play around and have some fun for the sake of your own sanity. And the most wonderful place to embrace this idea of childhood play is at the Museum of Toys and Play in Kielce. Located in a historic 19th century building, you'll get to see Polish folk toys, vintage Barbie dolls, miniature train sets, theatre puppets, and loads more playful goodness besides.

(plac Wolności 2, 25-367 Kielce; www.muzeumzabawek.eu)

59. Take in Some Polish Opulence at Rogalin Palace

Fancy getting off the beaten track while you're in Poland? Well, we think that the small village of Rogalin in the north of the country is well worth a visit. But this is no ordinary village, because it plays host to an incredibly grand palace, which was built by an aristocratic family in the late 18th century. As well as the grand opulence of the structure itself, we suggest checking out the gallery inside and its impressive collection of paintings.

(Arciszewskiego 2, 62-022 Rogalin; http://rogalin.mnp.art.pl)

60. Party With Friends at the Annual Woodstock Festival

Woodstock Festival is, of course, a world famous event that takes place in the United States, and played a huge part in the free love movement. Well, did you know that Poland has its own inspired Woodstock Festival? Now you do! And believe us when we say that this festival is a big deal and you need to make an effort to go. Up to 750,000 people attend each year, and it's totally free to attend! Acts that have performed include The Prodigy and Papa Roach.

(http://en.woodstockfestival.pl)

61. Shop for Fresh Foods at Wroclaw's Market Hall

When in Wroclaw, visiting the Market Hall is an absolute must. It has an elegant structure, and dates back to the early 20th century, but it's what's sold inside that really gets us excited. This is a place where you can find all kinds of delicious Polish nibbles. Just right of the entrance is a no-fuss and totally fantastic pierogi bar. You'll also find an abundance of cheeses, cured meats, teas and coffees, and loads more for an indulgent shopping and eating experience.

(Piaskowa 17, 50-359 Wrocław)

62. Visit the Largest Castle in the Whole World

Have you heard of Malbork in Poland? We totally are not going to judge you if you haven't because it's not one of Poland's well known tourist spots, and yet it is home to the largest castle in the whole world. Yes, in the whole world. This magnificent structure was originally built by Teutonic Knights way back in the 14th century, and eventually became a Royal residence. Since the castle is so big, it's a good idea to hire a tour guide who can show you the highlights.

(Starościńska 1, 82-200 Malbork; www.zamek.malbork.pl)

63. Escape City Life at Oliwa Park

Gdansk is a city that is absolutely packed full of charm, and since it's one of the country's smaller cities, it doesn't get too hectic. But if you'd still like to escape city life for a while, you can always find your way to the delightful Oliwa Park, which covers 10 hectares of green space in Gdansk. There is so much to explore once you get inside: a palm house, botanical gardens, and even a Chinese garden when you can find total peace and tranquillity.

(Opacka, 80-338 Gdańsk;

www.parkoliwski.gdansk.pl/ chapter_76534.asp)

64. Pick up Some Porcelain in Boleslawiec

If you are an artsy person, make sure that you can tear yourself away from the major galleries for a day so that you can visit a charming Polish town called Boleslawiec, which is best known for its 350 year commitment to producing wonderful ceramics. All of the pottery has the distinctive colours of creamy white and royal blue. Be sure to walk around and pop into some of the ceramics studios to see the local artisans at work.

65. Have an Artsy Day at Warsaw's Centre for Contemporary Art

When you think of the most famous arts centres in Europe, you would probably think of places like Florence and Paris, but believe it or not, there's also a thriving arts culture in Warsaw. At Warsaw's Centre for Contemporary Art, you'll feel the pulse of the city's creativity. There are many rotating exhibitions, and you can find everything from paintings to video installations, and sculptures to performance art.

66. Enjoy the Unique Flavours of Golabki

When you think of Polish food, what is the first thing that comes to mind? Probably pierogis, right? But there is so much more to Polish cuisine than just this, and one of our favourite dishes is most definitely Golbaki, which are cabbage rolls that are stuffed with meat and rice or barley, and then served hot in a creamy tomato sauce. They are particularly popular during Christmas time.

67. Visit the Largest Brick Church in the World, in Gdansk

If you're a fan of church architecture, you will certainly not be disappointed on your trip to Poland, and it's in Gdansk that you'll find a very unique church indeed. St Mary's Church is unique because it is made completely from bricks. Not only that, but it's actually the largest brick church to be found anywhere in the world. Be sure to climb the 405 steps of the church tower for the most breath taking viewing across the coastal Polish city.

(Podkramarska 5, 80-834 Gdańsk; https://bazylikamariacka.gdansk.pl)

68. Sip on Delicious Hot Chocolate at Krakow's Choco Café

If you find yourself in Krakow on an overcast day, and you want something to warm you up and make you smile, we can think of nothing better than a silky smooth cup of hot chocolate from Krakow's Choco Café. The chocolate is rich and perfectly indulgent, and since they are open until 11pm, you can also make it your go-to place for a bit of late night decadence.

(Wiślna 8, 31-007 Kraków; www.chococafe.pl/en)

69. Take in the View from Wroclaw's Sky Tower

You would no doubt expect the tallest building in Poland to be found in the country's capital city, when actually it's a pretty recent addition to the skyline of Wroclaw. This building is virtually a city itself, with apartments, shops, offices, and restaurants inside. But what we love most about the Sky Tower is its viewing point all the way up on the 49th floor, which is the highest panoramic viewpoint in all of Poland.

(Powstańców Śląskich 95, 53-332 Wrocław)

70. Shop for Amber While in Gdansk

While you're in Poland, you'll no doubt want to shop for some special items so that you can always remember your magical time in the country, and we can think of nothing more special than amber jewellery from Gdansk. It's a well kept secret that Gdansk is actually the amber capital of Europe, and you can find some incredibly beautiful jewellery there. Mariacka Street in the Old Town is filled with quaint, family run amber jewellers.

71. Take in all the Glory of Poznan Cathedral

We know that we've put a lot of cathedrals on this list, but honestly the amount of gorgeous, jaw dropping cathedral structures in Poland is just crazy. Poznan

Cathedral in the charming small city of Poznan is one of our favourites, and a lovely find in an off the beaten track place. The original structure was constructed way back when in 968, but has been remodelled numerous times since. The crypt is the oldest part of the cathedral that exists, so be sure to venture down there.

(Ostrów Tumski 17, 60-101 Poznań;
www.katedra.archpoznan.pl)

72. Find Peace at a Japanese Garden in Wroclaw

Wroclaw in Poland might just be the last place on earth that you would expect to find a perfectly manicured Japanese garden – but there it is! And when you need to escape city life, and enjoy some deep breaths in the fresh air, this is the place to find some zen. The garden dates way back to 1913, and contains a traditional Japanese carp pond, and gorgeous trees, plants, and flowers.

(Adama Mickiewicza 1, 51-618 Wrocław; www.ogrod-japonski.wroclaw.pl)

73. Try Traditional Foods at the Festival of Taste in Gruczno

Gruczno is a village in the north of Poland that you probably won't have heard about before, but there is one time of the year when it becomes a must visit destination for people all over Poland, and that's at the end of August when the village hosts the Festival of Taste. This is one of the largest food festivals in northern Poland, and it's a wonderful spot to get to grips with traditional food from this region, from pierogis to bigos, and much more besides.

74. Be Wowed by the Majesty of Lublin Castle

For fans of historic architecture, Lublin castle is a must visit spot. It was originally constructed way back in the 12th century, but has been added to and changed a lot since then. What makes this castle a special place is that it's here that the union with Lithuania was signed in the 16th century. Be sure to pay a visit to the Lublin Museum inside, which contains an impressive mix of folk art and weaponry.

(Zamkowa 9, 20-117 Lublin)

75. Find Vintage Treasures at Hala Targowa Market

While it's true that Krakow is a tremendously historic city, you are sure to notice that it's a city full of lots of cool looking people too. And in a place like Krakow, you can find plenty of flea markets and vintage stores where you can stock up on trendy clothes and cute items to take back with you. Our pick for the best flea market in Krakow would have to be Hala Targowa, a market that is open daily but has more selection on Sundays. Get there early for the best bargains.

76. Discover a World of Rural Polish Life at Skansen Museum

If you are the kind of person who gets totally bored when you walk from stuffy museum to stuffy museum, we think that Skansen Museum is the kind of museum that you might just like. This museum is located in the open-air, and everything is open to explore and not held behind glass partitions. This museum is dedicated to showing agricultural life from the 19th and early 20th centuries, with many recreated traditional buildings that you can enter. There's also a replica of a traditional market square.

(Aleksandra Rybickiego 3, 38-500 Sanok;
http://openairmuseum.pl/skansen/sanok)

77. Escape the Bustle of Wroclaw on Slodowa Island

One of the most charming things about Wroclaw city is the huge Oder river that passes through, and some of the islands that exist within this waterway itself. In fact, you can even visit one of these river islands: Slodowa Island. There are two pretty churches on the island, but what we love most of all is just walking around and feeling as though we are totally removed from all the stresses and responsibilities of everyday life.

78. Watch a Performance by the Warsaw Chamber Opera

If you're in Warsaw and looking for a reason to get all dressed up, what better reason than to take in a grand opera show? And we think that you can do no better than the Warsaw Chamber Opera, an opera company that has been operating since 1961, and puts on plays and concerts in an 18th century building. Their repertoire of performances is extremely varied, from Medieval mystery plays through to Baroque operas.

(aleja Solidarności 76B, 00-145 Warszawa; www.operakameralna.pl)

79. Indulge at Poland's Oldest Restaurant, Wierzyneck

For us, one of the best ways to get to know a new place is by eating as much of its delicious food as possible. So forget the pizza parlours and burger joints and head to some of the traditional eateries around Poland. And it doesn't get much more traditional than Poland's oldest restaurant, Wierzyneck in Krakow. This restaurant dates all the way back to the 14th century, and has served many a polish King in its time.

(Rynek Główny 16, 33-332 Kraków; www.wierzynek.pl)

80. Relax in the Colourful Main Square of Zamosc

If you have the time to veer away from the main tourist destinations in Poland for a while, be sure to check out a charming town in the south of the country called Zamosc, which is a perfect example of 16th century Renaissance town planning. The main square of this town is postcard perfect, with colourful charming arcaded burgher houses and the grand Town Hall. It's the perfect place to relax with a coffee and watch the world go by.

81. Indulge at the Annual Vodka & Snacks Festival

What's better than vodka? Errr, vodka accompanied by snacks. That's why we thank our lucky stars that Warsaw actually has a Vodka and Snacks Festival, which is hosted every May across a weekend. The festival boasts more than 200 varieties of vodka, and over 1000 different snacks, so that you can mix and match to find the perfect combination. There's also a cocktail bar to try out different vodka cocktails.

82. Camp on the Sand Dunes of Slowinski National Park

Nature lovers need to etch a trip to Slowinski National Park into their itineraries as a matter of priority. This park stretches along the Baltic coast in the northern part of Poland, and is most famous for its moving sand dunes, which can rise to up to 42 metres above sea level. They are truly something to behold, and we recommend camping on-site to take all the beauty of the park in. There is a campsite there so all you need is to pitch your tent and take in the serenity of the night stars.

(http://slowinskipn.pl/en)

83. Get Close to the Tallest Jesus Statue in the World

When you think of huge Jesus statues looming over the skyline, you would no doubt first think of Christ the Redeemer in Brazil. But believe it or not, there is an even larger Jesus statue in Poland. Christ the King can be found in Swiebodzin in the west of the country, and it is 33 metres tall, with a crown that takes up 3 metres alone. The statue was completed in 2010, and is the largest Jesus statue in the world.

(Sulechowska, 66-200 Świebodzin;
www.figurachrystusakrola.pl)

84. Kick Back and Watch a Movie at Kino Charlie in Lodz

There is absolutely no doubt that there is so much to see, do, and explore in Poland, and you don't need to have a down moment if you don't want it. But every now and then, it's great to kick back with a great movie, even when you are discovering a foreign country, and when that moment comes, be sure to check out Kino Charlie in Lodz. This cinema is committed to underground, independent films, so it's also a good place to meet some hipster locals.

(Piotrkowska 203/205, 90-451 Łódź; www.charlie.pl)

85. Have a Rafting Adventure on the Dunajec River

The Dunajec River Gorge might just be the most beautiful gorge in all of Europe, but because it's not in Western Europe, not all that many people have heard of it. We think that the best way to take in all of that beauty is via a rafting trip, and there many tour companies who offer that activity. Around you will be the towering Pieneny and Tatra mountains, and nothing but cool water beneath. This is one that nature lovers shouldn't miss.

86. Take in an Organ Concert at Oliwa Cathedral

Gdansk is a very attractive city, and it's Oliwa Cathedral, the main cathedral in Gdansk, that takes centre stage. Not only is this cathedral extremely beautiful, but it has one of the most impressive organs in any church we have visited. The organ itself dates all the way back to the 18th century, and it has earned a reputation for its incredible tone. The church hosts 20 minute organ performances six times a day, so there is no excuse not to catch a show.

(Biskupa Edmunda Nowickiego 5, 80-330 Gdańsk;
www.archikatedraoliwa.pl)

87. Start Your Day Right at the Breakfast Market of Warsaw

As the saying goes, breakfast is the most important meal of the day, and so what better place to start a Polish morning than at the Breakfast Market in Warsaw? It's only open on a Saturday, and as probably will have guessed, the morning time is most definitely when to be there. Many local producers serve up all kinds of local and international treats, and it's a very charming spot to be when the sun is shining and with a pastry in hand.

(aleja Wojska Polskiego 1, 00-001 Warszawa)

88. Enjoy the Open-Air Festivities of St Dominic's Fair in Gdansk

St Dominic's Fair in Gdansk is a big deal. Like, 750 years of history big deal. That's right, the first time the fair took place was in the year 1260, when it was established by the Pope at the time, and it has gone on to become one of the largest and most important open-air cultural events in Europe. Believe it or not, 5 million people come and go Gdansk to enjoy this important event, its incredible funfairs, street food, flea markets, and more. It can last for up to three weeks, and takes place in August each year.

89. Go Underground at Paradise Cave

Have something of an adventurous spirit? Then make sure that you explore the underground world of Poland, and find your way to the Paradise Cave. This limestone cave is located inside the Malak Hill, and although it's not a large cave, it's considered to be one of the most beautiful in Poland. Explore the five chambers, and you'll be transported to a world of stalagmites, stalactites, and speleothems.

(Dobrzączka, 26-060 Chęciny; http://jaskiniaraj.pl/en)

90. Cool Down With an Ice Cream From Lodziarnia Donizetti

Okay, we know that Poland isn't an exotic destination with a year round tropical climate, but if you find yourself in Krakow in the summer months, and you are looking for a way to cool down, ice cream is always the answer. And for our money, the best ice cream spot in Krakow is Lodziarnia Donizetti. All of their unique flavours are handmade, and there is always something different and delicious to try. We particularly enjoy the chestnut and cherry flavours.

(Świętego Marka 23, 30-001 Kraków)

91. Explore an Ancient Settlement in Biskupin

There is plenty for history lovers to explore in Poland, but there's more than grand castles and museums. One of the most underrated but fascinating places would have to be Biskupin, an open-air archaeological site that you can explore. This Iron Age fort is known as the Polish Pompeii and is the most interactive archaeological site in Europe. The original village of Biskupin dates all the way back to the 5th century BC.

(www.biskupin.pl)

92. Take in Modern Polish Art at Wroclaw Contemporary Museum

Located in the Old Town of Wroclaw is a former air raid shelter, which has undergone a really extraordinary renovation to become the premiere contemporary art museum in the city. This museum is primarily dedicated to works of art from the 20th century, with a very strong focus placed on local artists from Wroclaw. There's always temporary exhibits, so there's always something new to check out.

(Bunkier/ schron przeciwlotniczy, plac Strzegomski 2a, 53-681 Wrocław; http://muzeumwspolczesne.pl/mww/?lang=en)

93. Get to Grips With Polish Gold Mining in Zloty Stok

Did you know that there are some places in Poland that have been mining gold for centuries upon centuries? Zloty Stok is one of those places, and if you make it to this town, it can be a really great idea to explore the actual goldmine. There are 129 underground corridors, so there is plenty to explore, and if you really want a thrilling experience you can take a boat ride on the flooded underground passage of the Gertrude Mineshaft.

94. Take in the Street Art of Warsaw

Poland is a country with a surprisingly great arts culture, but you can do one better than traipsing from gallery to gallery. If you really want to get to know the art of the people, you need to take to the streets and check out the rich street art culture. And Warsaw is a country with plenty of street art. You can find it by looking around yourself, but it's a great idea to take a tour so that you can better understand the ideas behind the art.

95. Party and Meet Locals at Frantic Club, Krakow

If you're the kind of person who loves to party until the early hours of the morning, you are certainly going to the right place, and one of our favourite places to dance with locals in Krakow is Frantic Club. They attract some of the best DJ talent from around Europe, and really pump out those tunes with a fantastic sound system. Just don't drink too much vodka!

(Szewska 5, 31-000 Kraków; www.frantic.pl)

96. Take a Boat Trip to a Riverbank Village

Krakow is a really fun city, but there's also some great stuff nearby for day trips. Tyniec is a village along the river Vistula that is just 12 km outside of Krakow and you can get there on a charming boat trip along the river. This quaint village is famous for its Benedictine Abbey that was founded all the way back in the 11th century by King Casimir the Restorer. We recommend hiring a guide if you really want to experience the best of the abbey.

97. Take in a View of Wroclaw From the Penitent Bridge

One of the most beautiful structures in Wroclaw is certainly the Mary Magdalene church. This church has two big red towers that dominate the cityscape, and there is also a bridge that connects the two of them at a height of 45 metres. If you're a sucker for a view, it's a really great idea to spend some time on this bridge while taking in an epic view of all Wroclaw city around you.

98. Keep Kids Happy at the Copernicus Science Centre

Travelling with kids is no easy task. They demand to be entertained at all times, but we think that the Copernicus Science Centre in Warsaw is somewhere they'll have a great time while learning something new. This is one of the most advanced science museums in Europe, and the point of difference is that almost all the 450+ installations are totally interactive, so you and your kids can actually carry out science experiments yourselves.

(Wybrzeże Kościuszkowskie 20, 00-390 Warszawa; www.kopernik.org.pl)

99. Unwind in the Malta Thermal Baths in Poznan

There's a lot to see and so in Poland, but make sure that you also take the time to relax and unwind on your trip, and we can think of no better way to do so than to take a dip in the Malta Thermal Baths in the small city of Poznan. And there really is a lot to explore: an Olympic sized pool, a waterpark with 16 slides, a World of Saunas with 14 saunas, and a spa area with underground springs, massages, hammams, and more. *(Termalna 1, 61-028 Poznań; www.termymaltanskie.com.pl/en/)*

100. Eat Lots of Yummy Krakowska Sausage

Something that you are sure to notice during your time in Poland is that the local people certainly do like to eat meat. And with yummy treats like the Karakowska sausage, who on earth could blame them for that? It is made from lean cuts of pork, seasoned with pepper, allspice, coriander, and garlic, and then smoked. As you can probably tell from the name, the place to find this sausage is Krakow.

101. Have a Surreal Experience at the Dalineum

Poznan is probably the last place you would think to find a gallery dedicated to the Spanish surrealist, Salvador Dali, but there it is, and this quaint place is a very welcome, if somewhat random, addition to the city's gallery scene. This private collection contains a number of paintings, ceramic sculptures, and metalworks, and all inside a windowless building to add that extra sense of off-kilter surrealism.

(Wielka 24, 60-101 Poznań)

Before You Go...

Thanks for reading **101 Coolest Things to Do in Poland.** We hope that it makes your trip a memorable one!

Keep your eyes peeled on www.101coolestthings.com, and eat lots of pierogis during your trip!

Team 101 Coolest Things

Made in the USA
Lexington, KY
11 February 2018